Traditional Celebrations

Ian Rohr

A+

Smart Apple Media
P.O. Box 3263
Mankato, MN, 56002

First published in 2010 by
MACMILLAN EDUCATION AUSTRALIA PTY LTD
15–19 Claremont St, South Yarra, Australia 3141

Visit our web site at www.macmillan.com.au or go directly to www.macmillanlibrary.com.au

Associated companies and representatives throughout the world.

Library of Congress Cataloging-in-Publication Data

Rohr, Ian.
Traditional celebrations / Ian Rohr.
p. cm. -- (Celebrations around the world)
Includes index.
ISBN 978-1-59920-540-3 (library binding)
1. Holidays--Juvenile literature. I. Title.
GT3933.R636 2011
394.26--dc22

2009042146

Publisher: Carmel Heron
Managing Editor: Vanessa Lanaway
Editor: Michaela Forster
Proofreader: Kirstie Innes-Will
Designer: Kerri Wilson (cover and text)
Page layout: Pier Vido
Photo researcher: Wendy Duncan
Production Controller: Vanessa Johnson

Manufactured in China by Macmillan Production (Asia) Ltd.
Kwun Tong, Kowloon, Hong Kong
Supplier Code: CP January 2010

Acknowledgments
The author and the publisher are grateful to the following for permission to reproduce copyright material:

Cover photograph: Children dressed up for Halloween,© Ariel Skelley/The Image Bank/Getty Images

© Gideon Mendel/Corbis, **17**; © Dreamstime, **18**; © Dreamstime/Kristian Sekulic, **14**; © Blue Jean Images/Getty Images, **13**; © Leland Bobbe/Getty Images, **11**; © Brand New Images/Stone/Getty Images, **5**; © Michael Dunning/Getty Images, 10; © Ezio Geneletti/Getty Images, 9; © Peter Macdiarmid/Getty Images, 7; © Hiroko Masuike/Getty Images, **8**; © Dario Mitidieri/ The Image Bank/Getty Images, **6**; © Mike Powell/Allsport/Getty Images, **26**; © Ariel Skelley/The Image Bank/Getty Images, **1**, **19**; © iStockphotos/btrenkel, **25**; © iStockphoto/Jack Puccio, **21**; © iStockphoto/RonTech2000, **20**; Lonely Planet Images/Craig Pershouse, **22**; Lonely Planet Images/Anthony Plummer, **24**; MEA Images/Bananastock, **4**; photolibrary, **15**; Reuters/Todd Korol, **27**; Reuters/Vincent West, **28**, **29**; © Shutterstock/70sphotography, **12**; © Shutterstock/Creatista, **23**; © Shutterstock/Alexei Novikov, **16**; © Shutterstock/Kevin Renes, **30**.

While every care has been taken to trace and acknowledge copyright, the publisher tenders their apologies for any accidental infringement where copyright has proved untraceable. Where the attempt has been unsuccessful, the publisher welcomes information that would redress the situation.

Contents

When a word is printed in **bold**, you can look up its meaning in the Glossary on page 31.

Celebrations

Celebrations are events that are held on special occasions. Some are events from the past that are still celebrated. Others celebrate important times in our lives or activities, such as music.

Birthdays are special events that many people celebrate.

Some celebrations involve only a few people. Others involve whole cities or countries. Large celebrations take place across the world.

New Year's Eve is celebrated all around the world with fireworks.

What Are Traditional Celebrations?

Traditional celebrations are passed down from older people to younger people. Some are thousands of years old. Most countries have traditional celebrations.

There are many traditional celebrations held in European countries.

Traditional celebrations are held for many reasons. Most remember events from the past. Some have changed over time, while others are the same as they have always been.

Dragon and lion dances have been part of Chinese New Year celebrations for a long time.

New Year's Eve

New Year's Eve is celebrated on December 31. This is the last day of the year. It celebrates the end of one year and the beginning of the next.

People celebrate New Year's Eve in New York City's Times Square with balloons and confetti.

New Year's Eve has been celebrated for about 400 years. However, it dates back to **ancient** times. Over time, the date of New Year's Eve has changed.

New Year's Eve in 2000 was a large celebration to welcome a new century.

New Year's Eve celebrations have many traditions. These include fireworks displays, parties, and wishing people a "happy new year."

Large fireworks displays take place on Sydney Harbor in Australia.

On New Year's Eve, people try and start the new year in a happy way. They hope they will stay happy in the coming year.

Many people like to spend New Year's Eve with family and friends.

Chinese New Year

Chinese New Year is a big Chinese celebration. It is celebrated in China and in countries with large numbers of Chinese people. The celebrations include fireworks and parties.

Dragon and lion dances are a part of Chinese New Year celebrations in many countries.

Chinese New Year is based on a **lunar calendar**. The celebration date changes each year, but it is always in January or February.

Red envelopes containing money are given to children during Chinese New Year.

April Fools' Day

April Fools' Day is celebrated in many European countries on April 1. The **origins** of April Fools' Day are unknown. However, it has been celebrated for hundreds of years.

On April Fools' Day, many children have fun playing tricks.

On April Fools' Day, people play tricks on their friends. In some countries, jokes must be played before noon. In other countries, jokes are played all day.

People try to trick their friends on April Fools' Day.

May Day

May Day is a very old celebration. It is held in the **Northern Hemisphere** and celebrates the end of a long winter. It takes place on May 1 each year.

May Day is held when the trees start to blossom in the Northern Hemisphere.

On May Day, people dance around a **maypole** decorated with **garlands** and ribbons. The garlands are often made of blossoms. Another tradition is crowning the Queen of May.

Dancing around a maypole is a May Day tradition.

Halloween

Halloween is celebrated on October 31 each year. It is a very old festival, and it has many traditions. Today, Halloween celebrates scary things.

Carving a pumpkin into a lantern is a Halloween tradition.

Children dress up in scary costumes and go to houses to ask for treats. If they do not get a treat, they play a trick!

Children enjoy “trick or treating” at Halloween.

Thanksgiving, United States and Canada

Thanksgiving is a celebration that started in the United States and Canada. It was a time when people gave thanks for the **harvest**. The celebration is hundreds of years old.

People spend time with family and friends on Thanksgiving.

Today, Thanksgiving is a holiday in America and Canada. People share a special Thanksgiving dinner with family and friends.

Roast turkey is a traditional Thanksgiving Day food.

Festival of Yams, West Africa

The Festival of **Yams** is a harvest festival celebrated in West Africa. It is held in August at the end of the rainy season. The festival includes singing and parades.

Dancing is part of the Festival of Yams.

People thank their **ancestors** and the gods for a good harvest of yams. Yams are given to people in the villages.

Yams are a main harvest food in West Africa.

Chu Suk, Korea

Chu Suk is a Korean festival that celebrates the harvest and family. People leave rice and fruit at their ancestors' graves. They also have a special family feast.

Special rice cakes are eaten at the family feast.

A dance is held the night before Chu Suk. Women sing and dance in a circle. Other Chu Suk activities include wrestling, archery, and playing music.

Women wear traditional Korean clothes to the Chu Suk dance.

Calgary Stampede, Canada

The Calgary Stampede is a festival and **rodeo** held in Canada. It is celebrated in July for 10 days. Horse races and rodeo events are part of the festival.

Rodeo events are a big part of the festival.

Thousands of visitors from around the world come to take part in the festival. As well as the rodeo, there are horse races, dances, and parties.

Wagon races are popular at the Calgary Stampede.

Running of the Bulls,
Spain and France

The Running of the Bulls is held in Spain and France. Many bulls run through the streets of towns. People race in front of the bulls.

The most famous bull-running festival is in Pamplona in Spain.

Bull-running festivals have been held for hundreds of years. They are still very popular and many people come to watch.

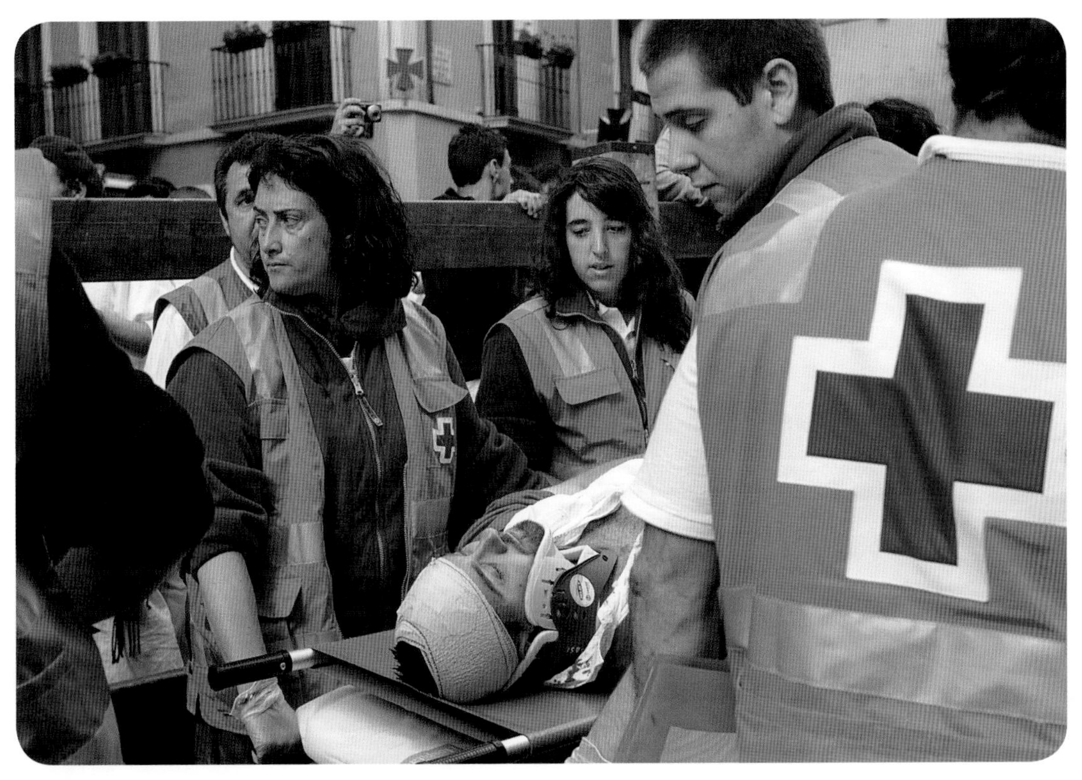

The running of the bulls can be dangerous, and sometimes people can get hurt.

Try This!

Try This Quiz

Find the answers to these questions in the book.
(You can check your answers on page 32.)

1. How long has New Year's Eve been celebrated?
2. What are given to children at Chinese New Year?
3. What type of festival is West Africa's Festival of Yams?
4. Where is Chu Suk celebrated?
5. Why do people celebrate May Day?

Try This Activity

Next time you celebrate a special occasion with your friends or family, ask yourself:

- Why are you celebrating?
- How long have people been celebrating this event?
- Are there other places in the world where people celebrate the event?

Glossary

ancestors	people who came before, such as grandparents and great-grandparents
ancient	happened thousands of years ago
garlands	flowers and leaves joined together
harvest	when the fruits and vegetables on farms are gathered or picked
lunar calendar	a calendar that is based on the movements of the Moon
maypole	a pole that is decorated with streamers
Northern Hemisphere	the countries and regions in the northern half of our planet
origins	the time when something first started
rodeo	an event that features cattle roping, bull riding, and horseback riding
yams	root vegetables, mostly grown in Africa

Index

Answers to the Quiz on Page 30

1. About 400 years
2. Red envelopes containing money
3. A harvest festival
4. Korea
5. To celebrate the end of winter

STAINS NOTED 3/18/19